WHAT DOES A
RUNNING BACK
DO?

Paul Challen

PowerKiDS
press

New York

Published in 2015 by The Rosen Publishing Group, Inc.
29 East 21st Street, New York, NY 10010

Produced for Rosen by BlueApple*Works* Inc.
Art Director: Tibor Choleva
Designer: Joshua Avramson
Photo Research: Jane Reid
Editor for BlueApple*Works*: Melissa McClellan
US Editor: Joshua Shadowens

Photo Credits: Cover, p.11, 17 James Boardman/Dreamstime; p. 1, 6, 8, 10, 13, 19, 21, 23, 24, 29
Andy Cruz; p. 3 Alhovik/Shutterstock, background Bruno Ferrari/Shutterstock; p.4, 14 Aspen
Photo/Shutterstock; p. 5, 7 Action Sports Photography/Shutterstock; p. 9 Richard Paul Kane/
Shutterstock; p. 12 Susan Leggett/Dreamstime; p. 15 Mike Liu/Shutterstock; p. 16 Eric Broder
Van Dyke/Shutterstock; p. 18 Haessly Photography/Shutterstock; p. 20 David Park/Dreamstime;
p. 22 Lawrence Weslowski Jr/Dreamstime; p. 25, 28 Ken Cole/Dreamstime; p 26 Scott Anderson/
Dreamstime; p. 27 Jerry Coli/Dreamstime

Library of Congress Cataloging-in-Publication Data

Challen, Paul C. (Paul Clarence), 1967–
 What does a running back do? / by Paul Challen.
    pages cm. — (Football smarts)
 Includes index.
 ISBN 978-1-4777-6994-2 (library binding) — ISBN 978-1-4777-6995-9 (pbk.) —
 ISBN 978-1-4777-6996-6 (6-pack)
 1. Running backs (Football)—United States—Juvenile literature. I. Title.
 GV954.C45 2015
 796.332'24—dc23

                                    2014001273

Manufactured in the United States of America

CPSIA Compliance Information: Batch #WS14PK8 For Further Information contact: Rosen Publishing, New York, New York at 1-800-237-9932

TABLE OF CONTENTS

THE FOOTBALL TEAM

Football teams are made up of an **offense** and a **defense**. Both parts of a team play very different roles, and both are crucial to a team's success. It takes a wide range of skills to play on both sides of the ball, including speed, strength, **agility**, and an ability to understand the patterns of the game.

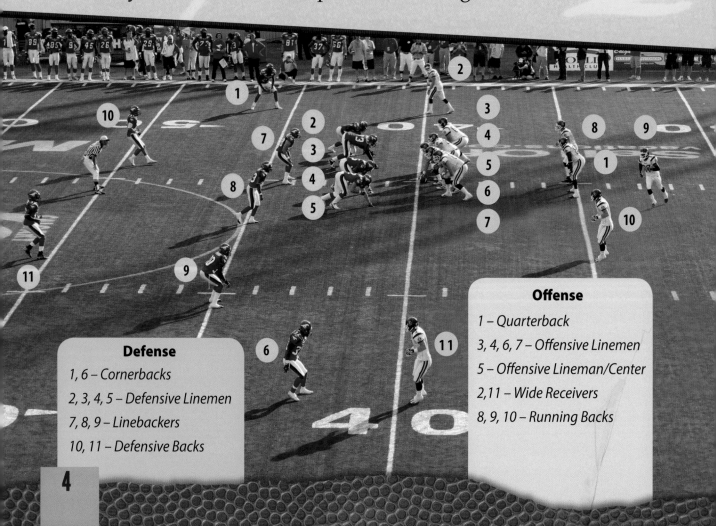

Defense
1, 6 – Cornerbacks
2, 3, 4, 5 – Defensive Linemen
7, 8, 9 – Linebackers
10, 11 – Defensive Backs

Offense
1 – Quarterback
3, 4, 6, 7 – Offensive Linemen
5 – Offensive Lineman/Center
2, 11 – Wide Receivers
8, 9, 10 – Running Backs

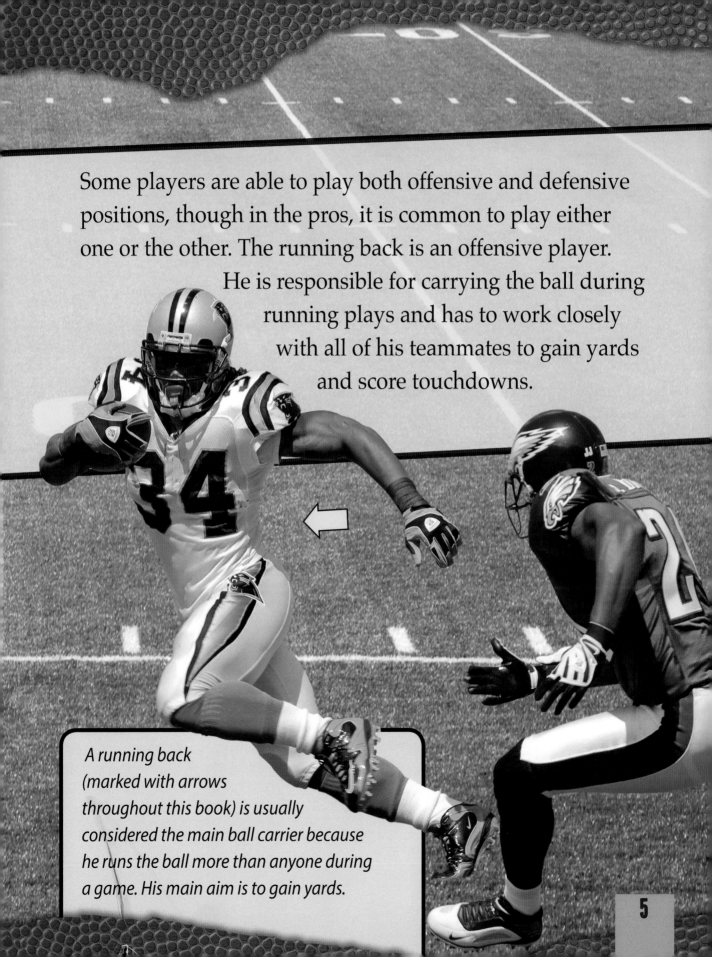

Some players are able to play both offensive and defensive positions, though in the pros, it is common to play either one or the other. The running back is an offensive player. He is responsible for carrying the ball during running plays and has to work closely with all of his teammates to gain yards and score touchdowns.

A running back (marked with arrows throughout this book) is usually considered the main ball carrier because he runs the ball more than anyone during a game. His main aim is to gain yards.

STRATEGY

When a football team has the ball, the offense must move it down the field using running or passing plays, and attempt to score a touchdown or kick a **field goal**. The defense tries to stop them. Both sides face off at the **line of scrimmage** on each play in a game.

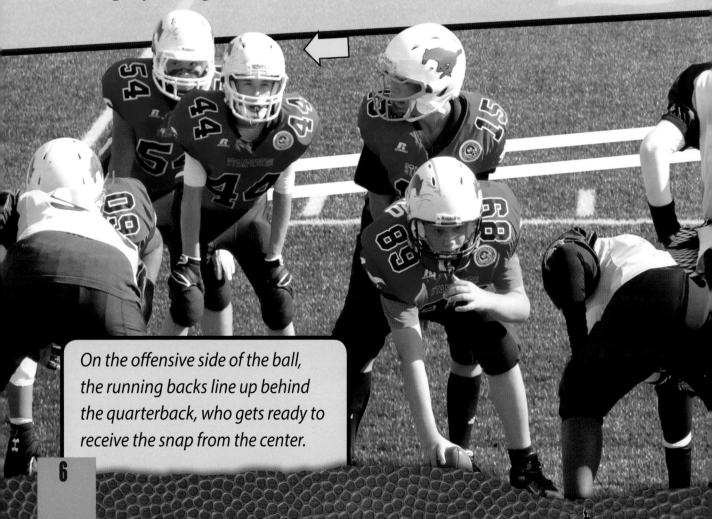

On the offensive side of the ball, the running backs line up behind the quarterback, who gets ready to receive the snap from the center.

Offensive players need skills like throwing, running, catching, and blocking. When an offense sets up to play, it usually features pass-catchers (receivers), players who run with the ball (running backs), and **blockers** (the offensive line). When the ball is snapped from the **center** to the quarterback, running backs become involved in the play as ball carriers or blockers for their teammates.

The best running backs are very fast on their feet. They need to be able to outrun their opponents.

STANCE AND START

A running back needs to be ready to get involved in the offense as soon as the ball is snapped, whether it's to block, receive a **hand off**, or catch a pass. So it's important that he uses a good **stance** to prepare himself when the team lines up. A running back uses either a two-point or three-point stance.

The running backs get set in the two-point stance to receive a hand off, block for teammates, or run a pass route.

In the two-point stance, he places his feet about shoulder width apart and bends his knees slightly, balanced and ready to spring. In the three-point stance, he goes into a crouch and places one hand forward, leaning towards the line of scrimmage. This body position allows him to burst out of his stance quickly when the ball is snapped.

Using a three-point stance in the backfield, a running back is ready to explode with speed and power when the ball is snapped.

When the quarterback receives the **snap** from the center, he often spins around to toss the ball to the running back. Sometimes called a pitchout, this allows a running back to catch the ball a few yards behind the line of scrimmage and get behind his blockers to make a run.

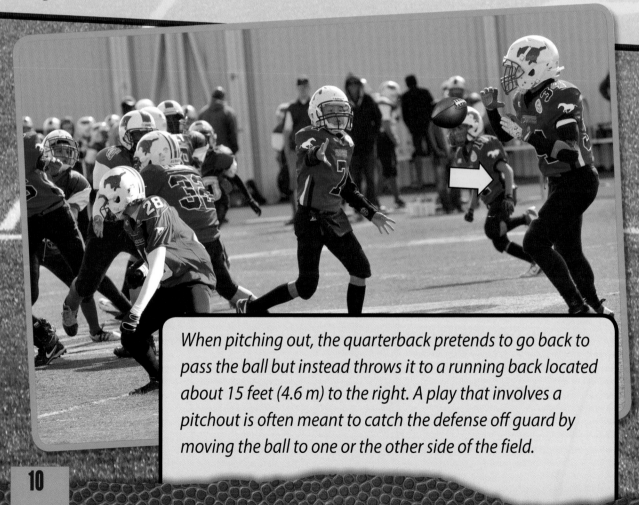

When pitching out, the quarterback pretends to go back to pass the ball but instead throws it to a running back located about 15 feet (4.6 m) to the right. A play that involves a pitchout is often meant to catch the defense off guard by moving the ball to one or the other side of the field.

The running back needs to be ready with **"soft hands"** to catch the ball without fumbling. It's also important for his timing with the quarterback to be just right, because the pitchout needs to get to the running back at a speed and angle that won't make him break his stride.

The pitchout requires great coordination and timing between the running back and quarterback. A proper grip on the football will help a running back to gain the most yards after the catch.

THE HAND OFF

Probably the most common running play is the hand off. This play looks simple enough, as the quarterback takes the snap, drops a step, and hands the ball to the running back. The running back then looks for holes in the defensive line to run through or runs to the outside looking for gaps.

A hand off is one of the actions that start a running play. The quarterback places the football into the stomach area of a running back. Once the ball is in his grasp, the running back runs to gain yards.

Sometimes running backs will confuse the defense by starting to run after a hand off or pitchout, and then throwing downfield to a receiver. This is called the run-pass. As long as the running back has not crossed the line of scrimmage, the rules permit him to throw to any eligible receiver—and that includes the quarterback! Of course, any team using this kind of play needs a running back with good throwing skills.

It is crucial that the running back gets his timing right with the quarterback on the hand off or a **fumble** can easily occur. Also, the running back must have his hands set so that when the quarterback hands him the ball, he can easily transfer it into one hand and start running.

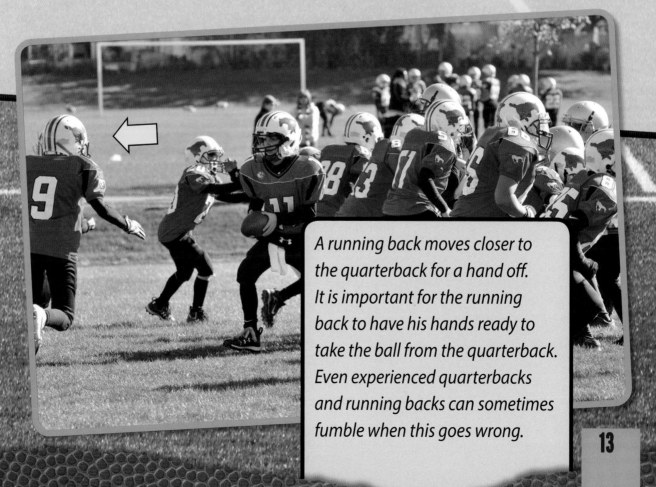

A running back moves closer to the quarterback for a hand off. It is important for the running back to have his hands ready to take the ball from the quarterback. Even experienced quarterbacks and running backs can sometimes fumble when this goes wrong.

CATCHING PASSES IN ZONES

As well as running with the ball after a hand-off or pitchout, running backs contribute to the offense as receivers. Because of this, they need good ball-catching skills.

An open receiver is a player who is not being guarded by a defensive player during a play. During a pass play, they tend to be downfield in one of the zones where a quarterback can deliver a pass to them. Open receivers have better chances to catch a pass from a quarterback and make big plays on offense.

Generally speaking, the short zone is the section of the field that's up to 5 yards in front of the line of scrimmage. The medium zone is from 5 to about 12 yards, and the deep zone is anything farther than that. As part of a team's offensive **strategy**, running backs will run routes into any or all of these zones to make a catch.

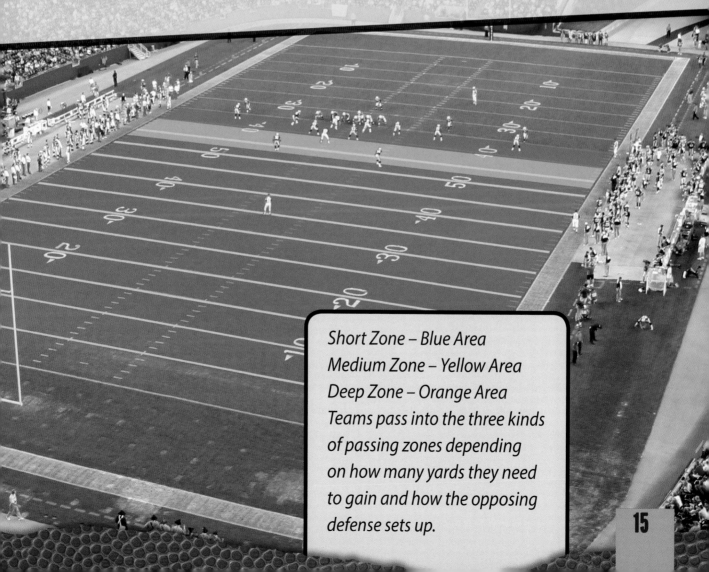

Short Zone – Blue Area
Medium Zone – Yellow Area
Deep Zone – Orange Area
Teams pass into the three kinds of passing zones depending on how many yards they need to gain and how the opposing defense sets up.

RUNNING PASS ROUTES

The pass route is the path a running back will take once the ball is snapped, as he tries to get open for a catch. These routes are almost always pre-planned, and offensive passing plays have several different receivers all running different routes.

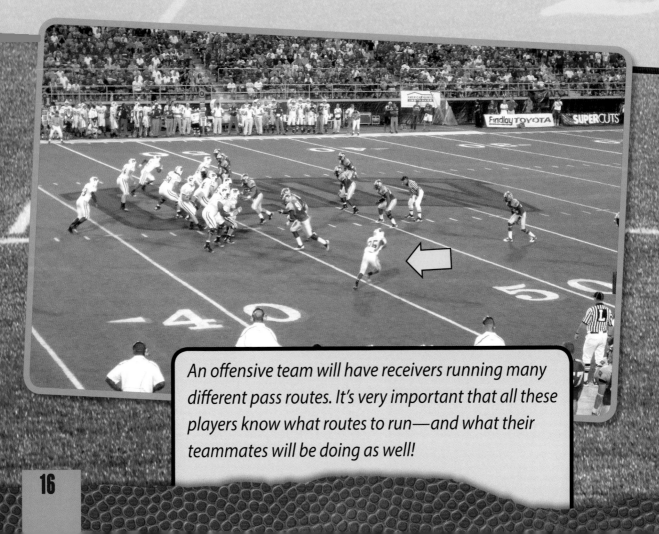

An offensive team will have receivers running many different pass routes. It's very important that all these players know what routes to run—and what their teammates will be doing as well!

Running an effective route is not all about the running back, though. He has to cooperate closely with the quarterback so that both players know in advance which routes are going to be executed. The quarterback will throw passes in many directions and distances to different players during a game. A good pass attempt will be directed downfield to an open receiver. With a combination of running backs and receivers running routes on any given play, it's important to avoid a collision.

The pass attempts carry a higher risk than a running play because the defense has the opportunity to intercept the ball in the air.

TYPES OF PASSES

Running backs often contribute to the offense as receivers. A running back can catch three basic kinds of passes: short, medium, and long. Sometimes, a team will need short yardage, so a receiver will be assigned to run into the short zone and look for a quick pass from the quarterback.

Running backs have to be able to catch all kinds of passes. Of course, there is always a defensive player looking to break things up!

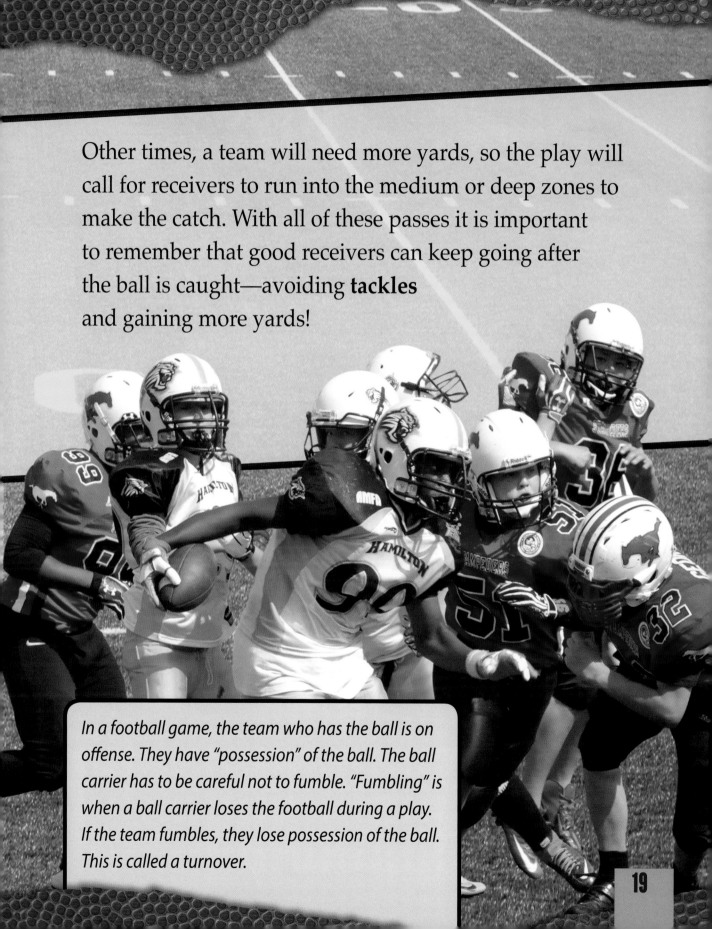

Other times, a team will need more yards, so the play will call for receivers to run into the medium or deep zones to make the catch. With all of these passes it is important to remember that good receivers can keep going after the ball is caught—avoiding **tackles** and gaining more yards!

In a football game, the team who has the ball is on offense. They have "possession" of the ball. The ball carrier has to be careful not to fumble. "Fumbling" is when a ball carrier loses the football during a play. If the team fumbles, they lose possession of the ball. This is called a turnover.

EVADING TACKLERS

No matter how a running back gets the ball, his main aim is to gain yards. Of course his defensive **opponents** are eager to stop him, and that's where the running back needs to use his physical ability and intelligence.

A tackle happens when the defensive players try to keep the offensive player from gaining any further yards. There are two kinds of tackles, "solo tackles" and "assisted tackles." Assisted tackles happen when more than one defensive player is involved in the tackle.

Running backs will use all kinds of moves and fakes to get past tacklers, cutting left and right and sometimes using sheer speed to get away. As well, good running backs know how to "break tackles" by pushing the defensive players away with their hands and arms, and keeping their feet moving.

Running backs can use a "straight arm" to push away a defensive player in an attempt to avoid being tackled.

BLOCKING

While running backs do seem to get a lot of a team's offensive glory by carrying or catching the ball to gain yards, their role also involves doing a lot of hard work in blocking for teammates. After all, only one player at a time can carry the ball, and the rest of the team needs to support him.

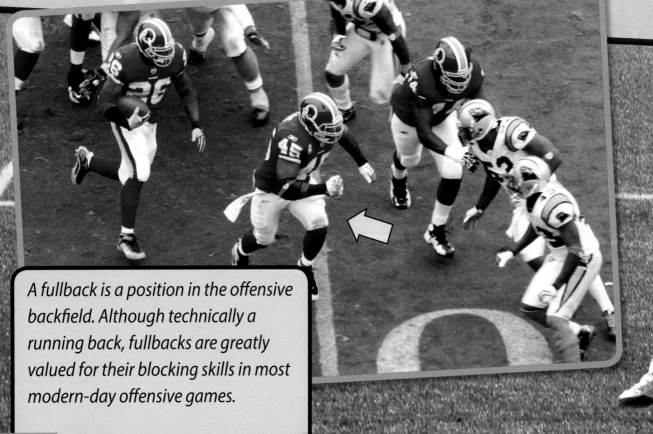

A fullback is a position in the offensive backfield. Although technically a running back, fullbacks are greatly valued for their blocking skills in most modern-day offensive games.

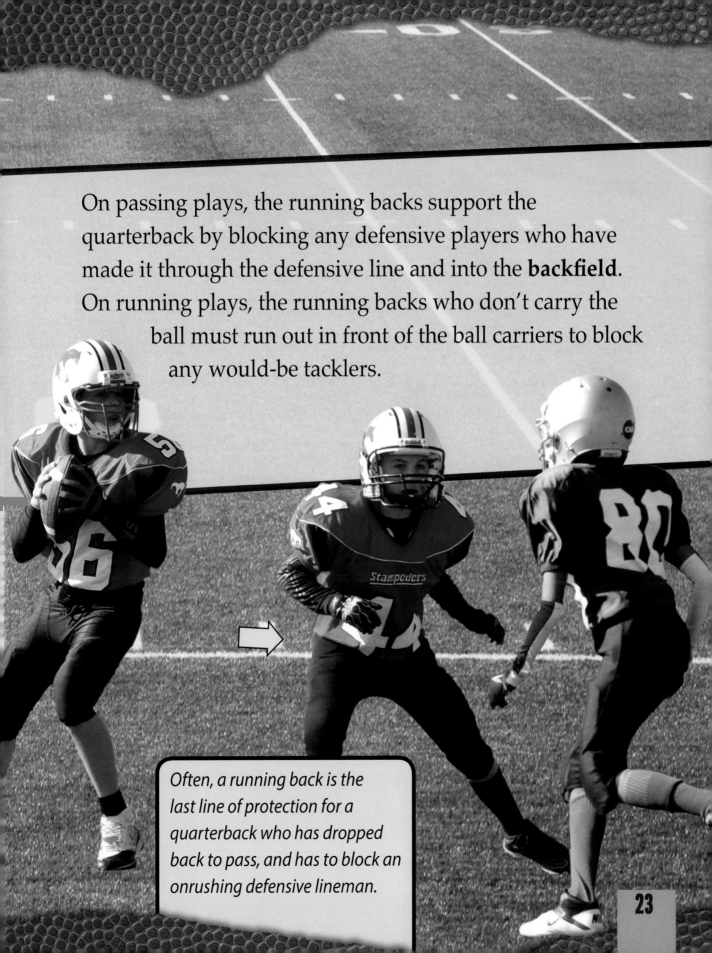

On passing plays, the running backs support the quarterback by blocking any defensive players who have made it through the defensive line and into the **backfield**. On running plays, the running backs who don't carry the ball must run out in front of the ball carriers to block any would-be tacklers.

Often, a running back is the last line of protection for a quarterback who has dropped back to pass, and has to block an onrushing defensive lineman.

THE COACH'S ROLE

The coach is the person who ties every aspect of a team together. He understands the importance of offense and defense, and knows how to balance both into a winning combination. The coach is also responsible for a team's overall strategy and for making decisions in the heat of a game.

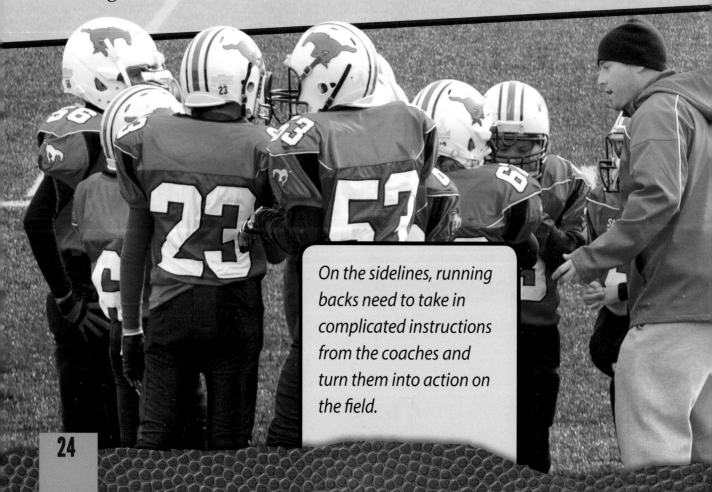

On the sidelines, running backs need to take in complicated instructions from the coaches and turn them into action on the field.

Every successful coach also knows that success in football comes from more than just developing skill on the field. Helping players get motivated, teaching an understanding of fair play and sportsmanship, and building a lifelong love of football are also very important.

Being a good coach is not only about teaching the game of football. Great coaches often play a role of a trusted advisers and friends to young players.

25

THE BEST RUNNING BACKS

Many great running backs throughout pro football history have thrilled fans with their speed, strength, and skills as varied as catching, blocking, and, of course, running with the ball. These include Franco Harris of the Pittsburgh Steelers, Tony Dorsett of the Dallas Cowboys, and O. J. Simpson of the Buffalo Bills. They all could break open a game and thrill a crowd with a single, spectacular run.

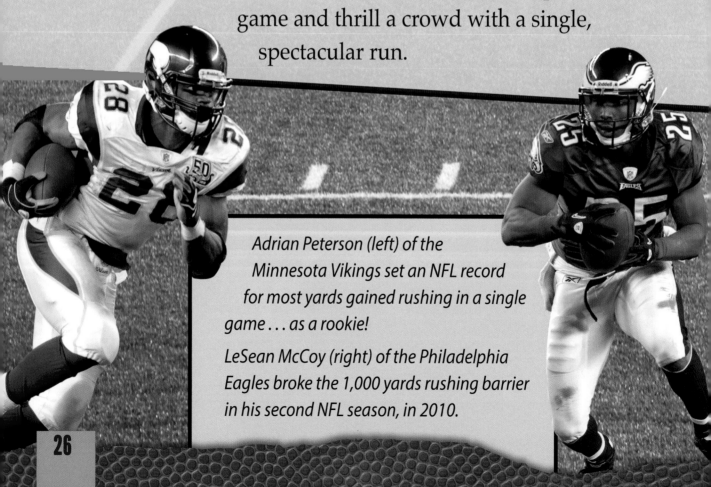

Adrian Peterson (left) of the Minnesota Vikings set an NFL record for most yards gained rushing in a single game . . . as a rookie!

LeSean McCoy (right) of the Philadelphia Eagles broke the 1,000 yards rushing barrier in his second NFL season, in 2010.

Many observers of the National Football League, consider Walter Payton, who played for the Chicago Bears from 1975 to 1987, to be one of the all-time greatest players in this position. Payton, who was known as "Sweetness," held several NFL records and invented several on-field moves, such as the "stutter-step," designed to confuse defensive players.

In recent years, Jamaal Charles, C. J. Spiller, Matt Forte, and Ray Rice have all been outstanding running backs and big-time fan favorites.

Emmitt Smith is the NFL's all-time leading rusher and played for three Super Bowl-winning Dallas Cowboys teams.

27

BE A GOOD SPORT

In the heat of a game, with the fans cheering and both teams trying to win, it is easy to lose your cool and react in a negative way towards the referees, your opponents, the fans, and even your coach. That's why it is important to remember that good sportsmanship is a very important part of football.

Good sportsmanship is built on respect for your opponents.

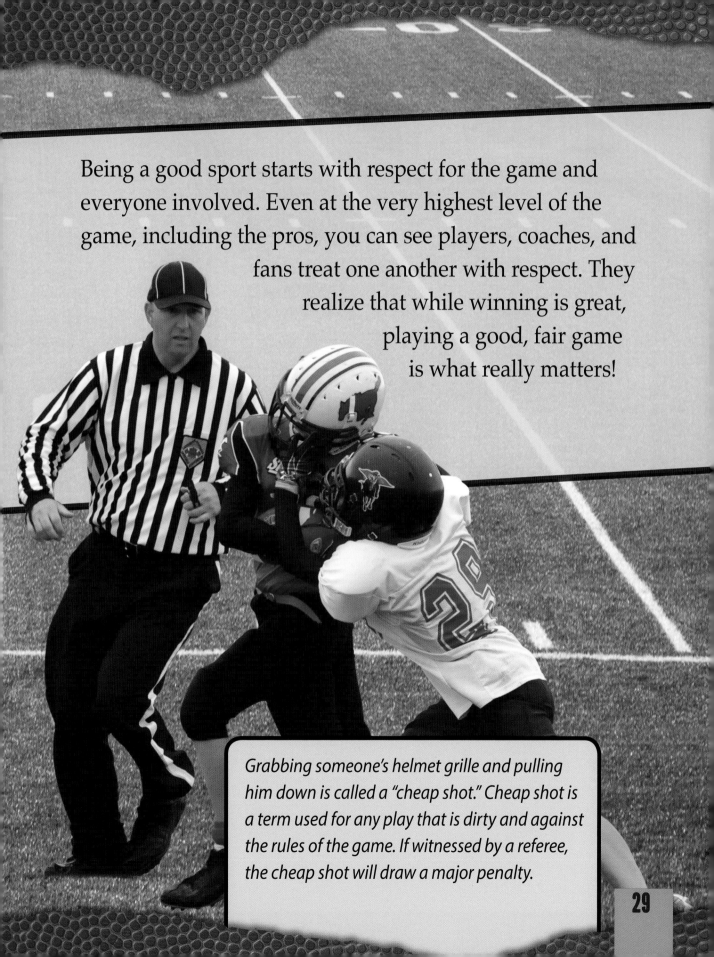

Being a good sport starts with respect for the game and everyone involved. Even at the very highest level of the game, including the pros, you can see players, coaches, and fans treat one another with respect. They realize that while winning is great, playing a good, fair game is what really matters!

Grabbing someone's helmet grille and pulling him down is called a "cheap shot." Cheap shot is a term used for any play that is dirty and against the rules of the game. If witnessed by a referee, the cheap shot will draw a major penalty.

GLOSSARY

agility (uh-JIH-luh-tee) Being able to move and change direction quickly and easily.

backfield (BAK-feeld) The area behind the line of scrimmage.

blockers (BLAH-kerz) Players who are trying to stop the other team's players.

center (SEN-ter) A player on the offensive line who snaps the ball to the quarterback.

defense (DEE-fents) Group of players trying to stop points from being scored by the other team.

field goal (FEELD GOHL) A play in which the ball is kicked through the uprights of the goalpost.

fumble (FUM-bul) Dropping the ball.

hand off (HAND OF) When one player hands the ball to another player during the play.

line of scrimmage (LYN UV SKRIH-mij) The invisible line where the ball was last down and where the next play starts.

offense (O-fents) Group of players trying to score points for their team.

opponents (uh-POH-nents) Another person or team you are competing against in a game.

soft hands (SOFT HANDZ) When catching the ball, the receiver's hands are relaxed not stiff so the ball doesn't bounce back out.

snap (SNAP) The action of the center tossing the ball between his legs to the quarterback.

stance (STANS) A way of standing.

strategy (STRA-tuh-jee) A type of clever plan.

tackles (TA-kulz) Knocks or throws another player to the ground.

FOR MORE INFORMATION

FURTHER READING

Edwards, Ethan. *Meet Arian Foster: Football's Ultimate Rusher*.
    All-Star Players. New York: PowerKids Press, 2014.

Frederick, Shane. *Football: The Math of the Game*. Sports Math.
    Mankato, MN: Capstone Press, 2012.

Kelley, K.C. *Running Backs*. Game Day: Football.
    New York: Gareth Stevens, 2010.

WEBSITES

Due to the changing nature of Internet links, PowerKids Press has developed an online list of websites related to the subject of this book. This site is updated regularly. Please use this link to access the list:

www.powerkidslinks.com/fbs/runb/

INDEX